Pizza

Written by Saturnino Romay

Illustrated by Annie Mitra

SCHOLASTIC INC.

New York   Toronto   London   Auckland   Sydney

Copyright © 1994 by Scholastic Inc.
All rights reserved. Published by Scholastic Inc.
Printed in the U.S.A.
ISBN 0-590-27362-0
ISBN 0-590-29213-7 (meets NASTA specifications)

1 2 3 4 5 6 7 8 9 10   08   01 00 99 98 97 96 95 94

Measure.

Pour.

Mix.

Roll.

Toss.

Stir.

Spread.

Chop.

Sprinkle.

Bake.

Smell.

Cut.

Eat!

Easy Pizza

Ingredients

Sliced English muffins

Tomato sauce

Shredded mozzarella cheese

1. Place English muffins on a cookie sheet.

2. Spread tomato sauce on top.

3. Sprinkle with cheese.

4. Bake at 350 degrees for ten minutes or until cheese is bubbly and golden brown.